A Note to Parents

DK READERS is a compelling reading programme for children. The programme is designed in conjunction with leading literacy experts, including Cliff Moon M.Ed., who has spent many years as a teacher and teacher educator specializing in reading. Cliff Moon has written more than 160 books for children and teachers. He is series editor to Collins Big Cat.

...ful illustrations and superb full-colour photographs co... with engaging, easy-to-read stories to offer a fresh app... to each subject in the series. Each DK READER is gu...ed to capture a child's interest while developing his o... ading skills, general knowledge and love of reading.

...ve levels of DK READERS are aimed at different re... abilities, enabling you to choose the books that are e... ight for your child:

P...l 1: Learning to read
Beginning to read
Beginning to read alone
Reading alone
...ving, re Proficient readers

The "normal" age at which a child begins to read can be anywhere from three to eight years old. Adult participation through the lower levels is very helpful for providing encouragement, discussing storylines and sounding out unfamiliar words.

No matter which level you select, you can be sure that you are helping your child learn to read to...

6 819 107 000

LONDON, NEW YORK, MUNICH,
MELBOURNE, and DELHI

DK UK

Series Editor Deborah Lock
Senior Art Editor Tory Gordon-Harris
Design Assistant Sadie Thomas
Production Claire Pearson
DTP Designer Almudena Díaz
Jacket Designer Peter Radcliffe

Reading Consultant
Cliff Moon, M.Ed.

Published in Great Britian by
Dorling Kindersley Limited
80 Strand, London WC2R 0RL

A Penguin Company
This edition, 2014

2 4 6 8 10 9 7 5 3 1
001—226833—February/2014

Copyright © 2003, 2014 Dorling Kindersley Limited

A CIP record for this book
is available from the British Library
ISBN: 978-1-4093-4258-8

Printed and bound in China
by South China Printing Company.

The publisher would like to thank the following for their
kind permission to reproduce their photographs:
(Key: a=above; c=centre; b=below; l=left; r=right t=top)

2 Tracy Morgan: (crb). **Ross Simms and the
Winchcombe Folk & Police Museum:** (cra). **Barrie
Watts:** (br). 4 Corbis: Jeremy Horner (c). 6–7 Getty
Images: Mike Timo. 7 Barrie Watts: (br). 8 Tracy
Morgan: (bl). Corbis: Bill Ross (cl). 8–9 Getty Images:
Darrell Gulin. 9 Natural History Museum: (bcr).
10–11 Getty Images: Jerry Driendl.
11 Stephen Oliver: (bc). 12 Stephen Oliver: (bc), (br).
13 Judith Miller & Dorling Kindersley & Bonhams,
Edinburgh: (bl). 15 Getty Images: Tom King (tr).
Stephen Oliver: (bc). 16–17 Gables Travels. 17 Guy
Ryecart: (bc). 18–19 Stephen Oliver. 19 Stephen Oliver:
(br). Natural History Museum: (bcl). 21 Corbis: Craig
Tuttle (br). 22 Ross Simms and the Winchcombe Folk &
Police Museum: (bl). 22–23 Jerry Young. 24–25 Jerry
Young. 25 Natural History Museum: (br). Jerry Young:
(c). 26 Stephen Oliver: (bl). 26–27 Getty Images: Terry
Husebye. 27 Getty Images: Paul Goff: (bl). 28 British
Museum: (br). 32 British Museum: (br).
Stephen Oliver: (c). Jerry Young: (bl)

All other images © Dorling Kindersley.
For further imformation see: www.dkimages.com

Discover more at
www.dk.com

Colourful
Days

blue

How many colours

green

yellow

pink

red

Come and
play with me.

can you see?

eye

nose

snow

white

6

We can play
in the cold,
white snow.

We can look at the purple flowers.

leaf

purple

flower

blossom

We can run
round the trees
with the pink
blossoms.

pink

petal

11

rabbit

 grey

ear

fur

We can play
with the small,
grey rabbits.

We can look
at the boats
on the blue sea.

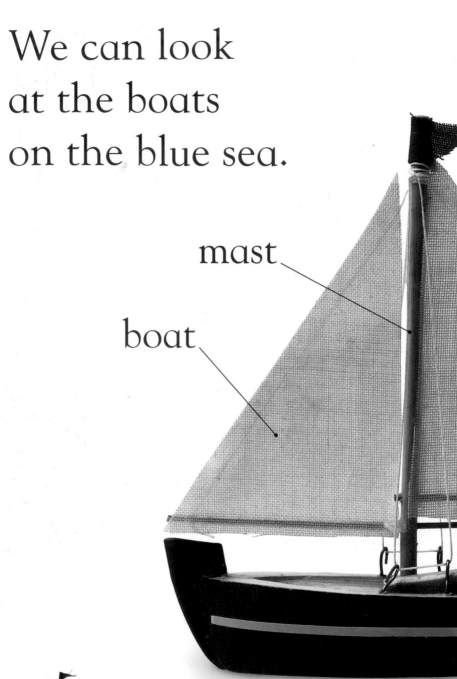

mast

boat

blue

sea

We can run
round the
tall, yellow
sunflowers.

yellow

sunflower

petal

 orange

We can
eat a cold,
orange lolly.

lolly

stick

leaf

red

We can kick
the red leaves and
pick the red apples.

apple

jaw

black

ant

beetle

We can look
at the ants and
the black beetle.

frog

feet

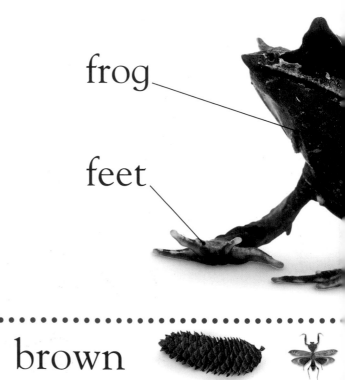

brown

We can croak
like the small,
brown frogs.

needles

tree

 green

We can run round
the tall, green trees.

We can hang up
silver balls and
put on gold crowns.

silver

ball

crown

jewel

 gold

How many colours

can you see?

Picture word list

white
page 6

purple
page 8

pink
page 10

grey
page 12

blue
page 14

yellow
page 16

orange
page 18

red
page 20

black
page 22

brown
page 24

green
page 26

silver and **gold**
page 28